HUNTING AND FISHING

GOING DEEP-SEA FISHING

BY FELIX PETERS

Gareth Stevens PUBLISHING

Please visit our website, www.garethstevens.com. For a free color catalog of all our high-quality books, call toll free 1-800-542-2595 or fax 1-877-542-2596.

Cataloging-in-Publication Data
Names: Peters, Felix.
Title: Going deep-sea fishing / Felix Peters.
Description: Buffalo, NY : Gareth Stevens Publishing, 2027. | Series: Hunting and fishing | Includes glossary and index.
Identifiers: ISBN 9781482482522 (pbk.) | ISBN 9781482482539 (library bound) | ISBN 9781482482546 (ebook)
Subjects: LCSH: Big game fishing--Juvenile literature.
Classification: LCC SH457.5 P484 2027 | DDC 799.16--dc23

Published in 2027
Gareth Stevens Publishing
2544 Clinton Street
Buffalo, NY 14224

Portions of this work were originally authored by Tyler Omoth and published as *Deep-Sea Fishing*. All new material in this edition was authored by Felix Peters.

Designer: Joshua Olson
Editor: Noah Riccardi

Photo credits: Cover, p. 1 Grzegorz Lukacijewski/Shutterstock.com; p. 4 John Scott Leigh III/iStockphoto; p. 6 Jodi Jacobson/iStockphoto; p. 8 Good Focused/Shutterstock.com; pp. 10, 20 Luna Marina/Shutterstock.com; p. 13 kelldallfall/Shutterstock.com; p. 14 temmuzcan/iStockphoto; p. 17 Przemyslaw Wasilewski/Shutterstock.com; p. 18 Cecop Alp/Shutterstock.com; p. 23 Wirestock Creators/Shutterstock.com; p. 24 Igor Zaytsev/Shutterstock.com; p. 27 AirLandSea/iStockphoto; p. 29 Ft. Laud/Shutterstock.com.

Printed in China.

CPSIA compliance information: Batch #QS27GS: For further information contact Gareth Stevens at 1-800-542-2595.

TABLE OF CONTENTS

CHAPTER 1

OPEN OCEAN FISHING

Deep-sea fishing is a kind of fishing that is done in water that is at least 100 feet (30 m) deep. People sometimes call it offshore fishing. Deep-sea fishing boats sail out to the deep waters of oceans and gulfs. The boats must be strong enough to handle strong waves and currents.

A fishing boat sails near Santa Catalina Island in California.

The mahi-mahi, sometimes called the dorado, is known for its bright colors.

People have gone deep-sea fishing for thousands of years. At first, people used hooks made of bone to catch fish. They sailed basic rafts. As people created better tools and boats, they could fish in deeper waters. Motorized boats allowed people to travel quickly. It became easier to reach good fishing spots.

Today, people can hire **charter boats** to take them out onto the water. They may also use **GPS** navigation to find their way around the oceans.

Deep-sea fishers, also called **anglers**, try to catch large fish that cannot be found near the shore. Popular types of fish include **mahi-mahi**, grouper, swordfish, and snapper. Anglers often eat the fish they catch. They may also make trophies.

FISHING DESTINATIONS

People travel all over the world in search of the biggest fish. Nova Scotia is known for its prized tuna. Giant blue marlins can be found in Australia, and Costa Rica is famous for its record-size mahi-mahis.

CHAPTER 2

FISHING GEAR

Deep-sea anglers try to catch large fish that can only be found in the open ocean. They need much stronger gear than people who fish in streams or lakes. Deep-sea anglers use heavy-duty fishing rods. These rods can withstand a fish's pulling. But they are also flexible.

Deep-sea fishing boats often have fishing rod holders.

Some anglers use special chairs for support as they reel in huge fish.

A reel at the base of the rod holds the fishing line. Deep-sea fishing line is strong and flexible. A float or bobber is attached to the line. It helps the line float in the water. This sets the depth of the bait or **lure**. Deep-sea anglers use large hooks to catch fish.

Many deep-sea fish are very heavy and very strong. They can pull the rod out of an angler's hands. To help reel in these fish, many anglers use a device called a fighting chair. This is a chair that can hold the fishing rod. It lets the angler sit down while fighting to pull the fish onto the boat. It can take over an hour to reel a fish in!

When an angler catches a fish, they must remove the hook from the fish's mouth. Many anglers use needle-nose pliers. This tool has a long, pointed nose. It keeps the angler's fingers safe while handling the sharp hook.

Many species of fish have weight limits. Anglers can keep only fish that are over a certain weight. A lip-grip scale allows anglers to weigh their catch right away. This scale can be hooked onto the fish's mouth. Some fish species may also have length requirements. For this reason, many anglers carry a tape measure. They use it to tell if a fish is the right size.

If the fish is big enough to keep, it can be prepared for storage. Many anglers use a long, thin knife called a fillet knife. They cut the fish's meat into narrow strips.

Sport fishers are people who go fishing just for fun. They do not eat the fish they catch. Instead, their goal is to enjoy the

A marlin's impressive size and speed make it an exciting catch for deep-sea anglers.

thrill of hooking a huge fish. Sport fishers often fish for sailfish and blue marlins. These fish are known as billfish. Sport fishers may even try to catch sharks.

CHAPTER 3

FINDING FISH

Before fishing, anglers study the kind of fish they hope to catch. This helps them choose the best bait to use. Anglers also look for places where fish tend to feed. Offshore structures such as **reefs** and canyons are good fishing spots. Even sunken ships can provide good places for fish to eat.

Many deep-sea anglers use mackerel as bait.

One of the best ways to find fish is to watch for signs above the water. When groups of birds gather on the open water, it usually means there are bait fish nearby. Areas with bait fish often have larger fish as well.

Modern equipment such as fish-finding devices can also help find good locations. These devices use **sonar** to show when schools of fish pass below boats.

There are three basic methods for deep-sea fishing. An angler chooses a method based on what type of fish they want to catch. They may also pick the best method for the area where they are fishing.

A group of birds flies over the water as an angler fishes for cod.

In one method, an angler lets the bait and line drag in the water behind the boat. This method is known as trolling. It is a good way to catch fast, aggressive fish.

Trolling is a good way to catch sailfish, wahoos, and tuna.

Trolling anglers often keep several lines in the water at one time.

Bottom fishing is another common method. In this method, an angler uses a sinker to weigh the line down. The sinker sits on the ocean floor while the bait and hook float nearby. Bottom fishing is a good way to catch fish that feed along the ocean floor.

The third deep-sea fishing method is called casting. An angler uses their fishing rod to throw the bait out on the water. Then they reel the line back toward the boat. The boat moves very slowly when an angler is casting. Sometimes it does not move at all.

Casting works well for fish that hide under structures such as rocks and reefs. Snappers and amberjacks are often caught using this method.

CHAPTER 4

STAYING SAFE

Every fishing boat should carry safety gear. There should be one life jacket for each person on board. Children should always wear their life jackets.

Flares are helpful, too. They can be used to signal other boats in case of emergency. Boats should also carry emergency position indicating radio beacons (EPIRBs).

Wearing a life jacket is an important part of water safety.

This device sends out a signal. It can tell rescue teams where to find the boat.

Before leaving for a deep-sea fishing trip, anglers should create a float plan. This plan tells where the boat will be going and what time it is expected to return. Anglers should share this plan with someone who is not going on the trip. That way, someone on shore always knows where the boat will be.

Fishing during storms and windy weather is dangerous. It is important for anglers to pay attention to weather forecasts. Boats should have radios on board. This allows anglers to monitor the forecast as the day goes on.

EPIRBs help rescue teams respond quickly or even find a boat's exact location.

The fish themselves can be dangerous, too. Some kinds of fish have sharp teeth. Others have poisonous stingers. Anglers should research the fish they hope to catch. They should study other common fish in the area, too. Learning the proper way to handle each kind of fish can help prevent injuries.

CHAPTER 5

RESPECTING NATURE

All deep-sea anglers must purchase fishing licenses. Money raised from the sale of fishing licenses is used to protect the fish's **habitats**. Anglers can help protect these habitats, too. They should avoid dumping litter or liquids into the water. Instead, they should throw away trash after they get back to shore.

Anglers can help protect fish and their habitats.

Anglers also need to know the size and quantity guidelines for the fish they catch. They should not keep fish that are too small. Releasing small fish helps more fish survive to become adults.

It is also important to handle fish as carefully as possible. Anglers must be gentle when removing hooks. They should

CIRCLE HOOKS

Most hooks are J-shaped. But circle hooks are less likely to harm fish. Their shape means they hook fish in the lip or jaw more often than J-shaped hooks. If a fish swallows a circle hook, it will not hook the fish's stomach. Instead, the hook will slide back out to the mouth. This protects the fish's organs.

An angler removes the hook from a marlin's mouth.

also be careful not to keep too many fish. By releasing any fish they do not intend to eat, anglers help make sure there will be plenty of fish in the future.

OFFSHORE WORLD CHAMPIONSHIPS

Talented anglers sometimes join competitions. At competitions, fishers try to score the most points. They get more points for rarer and larger fish. Top anglers can compete in championships. At these events, they often fish in teams.

The 2025 Offshore World Championships happened in Quepos, Costa Rica. It featured 158 fishers from 34 teams. Over three days, anglers caught and released 591 fish in total. They pulled in mostly sailfish as well as some marlin.

The winning team of anglers was Team Fish for Holly. Their leader was Captain Robert Collins. He had won the championship back in 2008. In 2025, his team pulled in 29 fish, scoring 6,100 points.

Bartels caught 16 sailfish (pictured) and one marlin during the three-day event.

The highest individual scorer was Catherine Bartels. She caught 17 fish and scored 3,500 points. That was 1,000 points more than the second-best fisher, Shaun Whale.

TEST YOUR KNOWLEDGE

Take this quiz to test your knowledge.

1. Write a paragraph describing the main ideas of Chapter 2.

2. Do you think conservation rules are too strict? Why or why not?

3. What do anglers use to weigh the fishing line down?

   A. a bobber
   B. a sinker
   C. a lure

4. Why would trolling not be a good method for catching bottom-feeding fish?

   A. Trolling does not use hooks.
   B. Trolling will not move the bait quickly enough.
   C. Trolling keeps the bait too high up in the water.

Answers can be found on page 32.

GLOSSARY

anglers
People who fish with a rod, reel, and line.

charter boats
Boats that can be reserved for private trips.

GPS
A navigation system that uses satellites to figure out location.

habitats
The places where plants or animals usually grow or live.

lure
An artificial bait used to attract and catch fish.

mahi-mahi
A large fish with a long fin along its back that is often caught by deep-sea anglers.

reefs
Ridges of sharp rock, coral, or sand just below the ocean surface.

sonar
A system for measuring distances and finding objects underwater by sending sound pulses.

FOR MORE INFORMATION

BOOKS

Brach, Kyle. *Deep-Sea Fishing*. Minneapolis, MN: Lerner Publications, 2024.

Parker, Madison. *Going Fishing*. Buffalo, NY: Rosen Publishing, 2026.

WEBSITES

Britannica Kids: Fishing
kids.britannica.com/students/article/fishing/274328
Learn more about fishing at this site.

PBS LearningMedia: Bass
thinktv.pbslearningmedia.org/resource/cc6cfdc0-dfde-44a5-95e4-facbdce89652/cc6cfdc0-dfde-44a5-95e4-facbdce89652/
Learn about bass, a popular fishing target.

Publisher's note to educators and parents: Our editors have carefully reviewed these websites to ensure that they are suitable for students. Many websites change frequently, however, and we cannot guarantee that a site's future contents will continue to meet our high standards of quality and educational value. Be advised that students should be closely supervised whenever they access the internet.

INDEX

Answer Key: 1. Answers will vary; 2. Answers will vary; 3. B; 4. C